learn to draw

Farm Animals

Learn to draw 21 favorite subjects, step by easy step, shape by simple shape!

Illustrated by Robbin Cuddy
Written by Jickie Torres

Associate Publisher: Elizabeth T. Gilbert
Art Director: Shelley Baugh
Managing Editor: Rebecca J. Razo
Associate Editor: Emily Green
Production Artists: Debbie Aiken, Rae Siebels

www.walterfoster.com
Walter Foster Publishing, Inc.
3 Wrigley, Suite A
Irvine, CA 92618

1 3 5 7 9 10 8 6 4 2

Table of Contents

Getting Started

When you look closely at the drawings in this book, you'll notice that they're made up of basic shapes, such as circles, ovals, and triangles. To draw all your favorite farm animals, just start with simple shapes. It's easy and fun!

Circles
are one way to start a pig's head, chest, and hips.

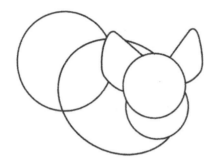 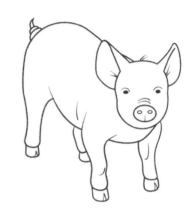

Ovals
are great for a rooster's head and body.

Triangles
are perfect for barns and roof tops.

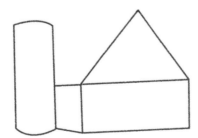 

Tools & Materials

Before you begin, gather some drawing tools, such as paper, a regular pencil, an eraser, and a pencil sharpener. For color, you can use markers, colored pencils, paint, crayons, or even colored chalk.

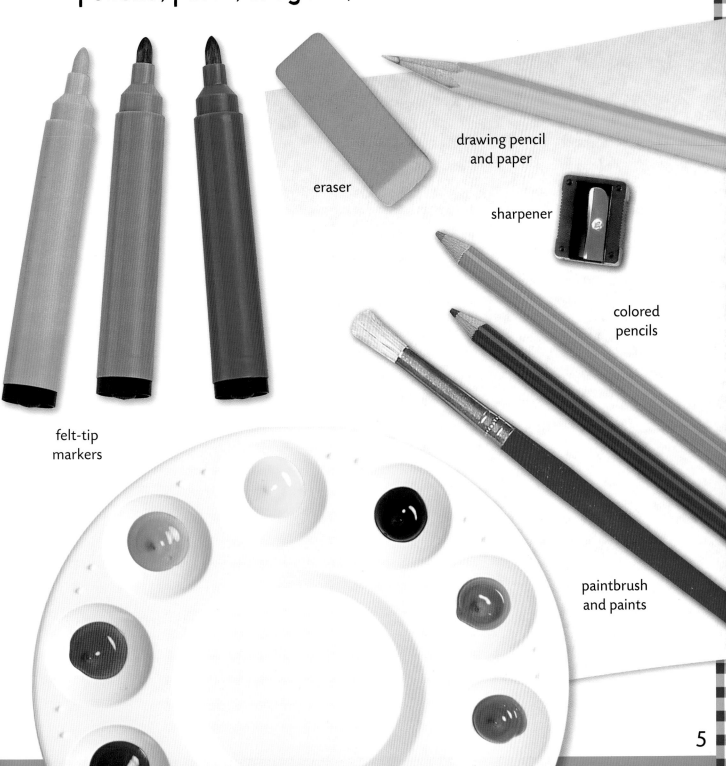

drawing pencil and paper

eraser

sharpener

colored pencils

felt-tip markers

paintbrush and paints

Cow

One of the largest animals on the farm, dairy cows produce milk. The most common dairy cow has a black-and-white pattern on its body. Others are brown and white, all brown, or all black.

5

6

Fun Fact

A dairy cow's milk goes further than the breakfast table. It is used to create a variety of products such as cheese, butter, yogurt, and ice cream!

Pig

Pink skin, a flat broad snout, and a curly tail are a few traits of the lovable pig. Pigs have small eyes and poor vision, so they use their snout to help them smell their surroundings.

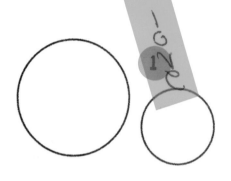

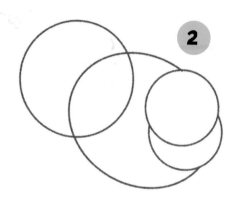

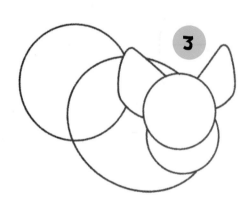

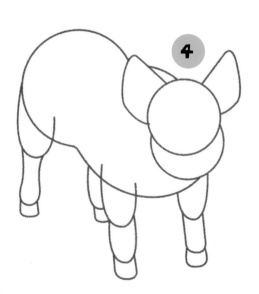

Fun Fact

Pigs don't sweat! To keep them cool in the summer, some farmers use sprinklers to mist them with water. Pigs will also roll around in mud to stay cool!

Bull

An adult male cow is called a bull.
The large, powerful bull has a wide head;
two large horns; and a broad chest.
Bulls are also more muscular than female cows.

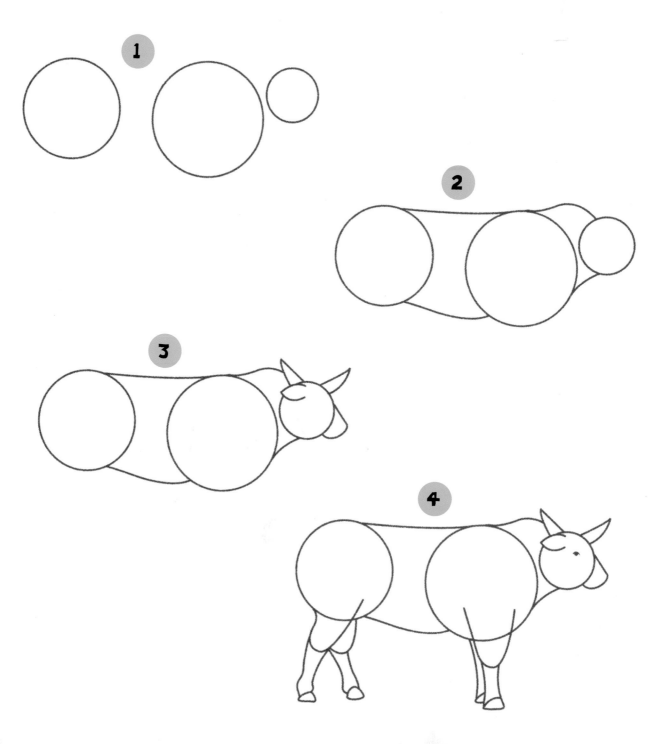

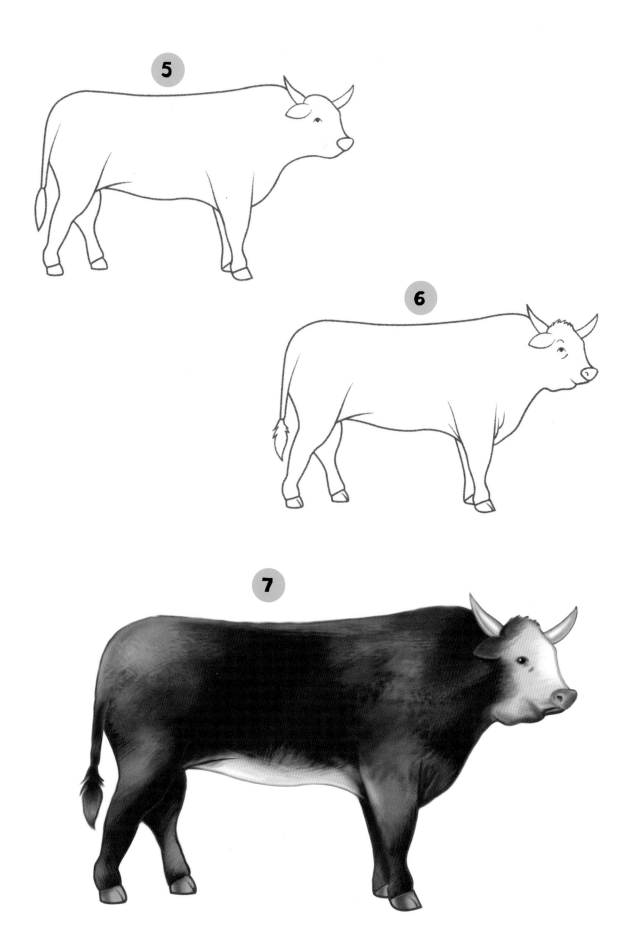

Sheep

Sheep have a thick coat used to create wool for blankets and other items. Farmers shave their sheeps' fleece in the spring. The sheep have the rest of the year to grow their fluffy coats back.

Fun Fact

A sheep's wool is naturally fire resistant. Wool is difficult to ignite because it needs extreme heat in order to burn. Because of this, wool is often used to make household carpets safer.

Horse

The graceful yet sturdy horse has a long, silky mane and a muscular body. Farmers ride horses for transportation, as well as to help them herd other animals.

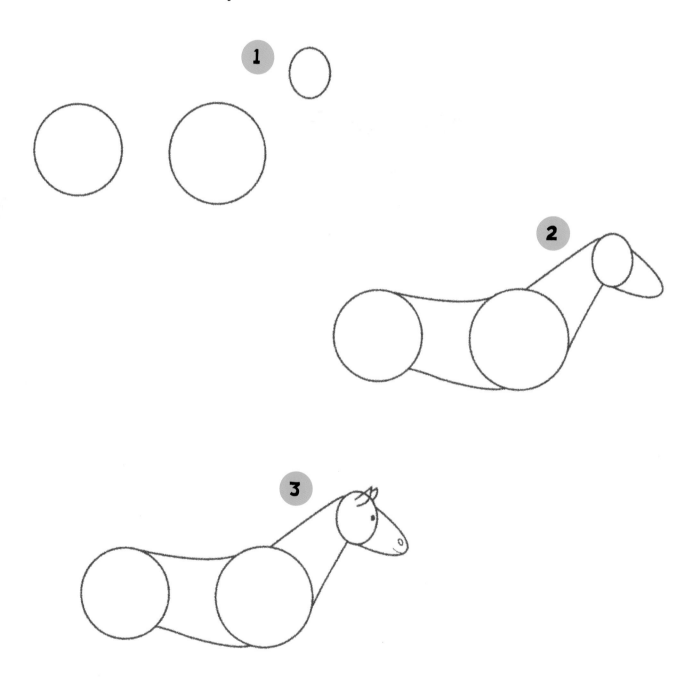

4

5

6

Goat

Farmers generally keep goats for their milk.
Goats are known for having long beards.
Female goats are called does,
and male goats are called bucks.

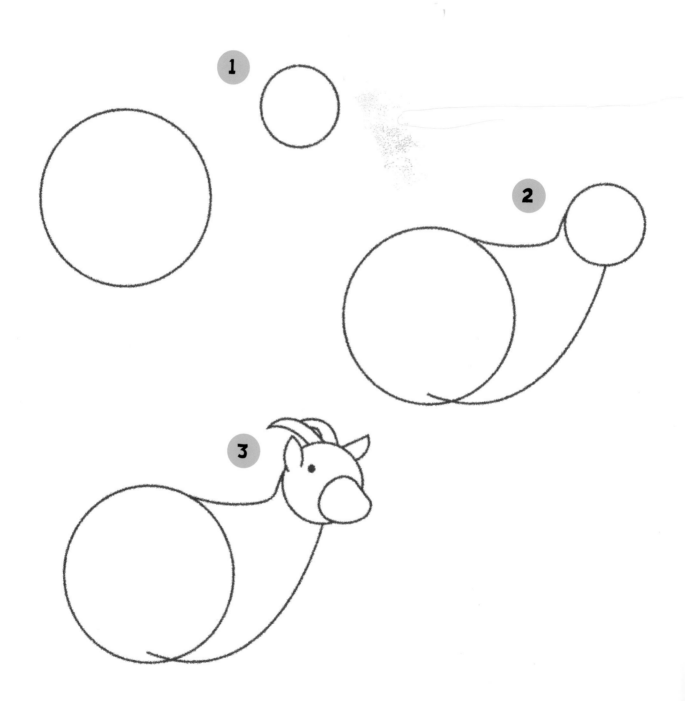

Donkey

Donkeys look similar to horses, but they are usually smaller with shorter, stockier legs and longer, wider ears. In some countries, donkeys are used to pull carts and plow fields.

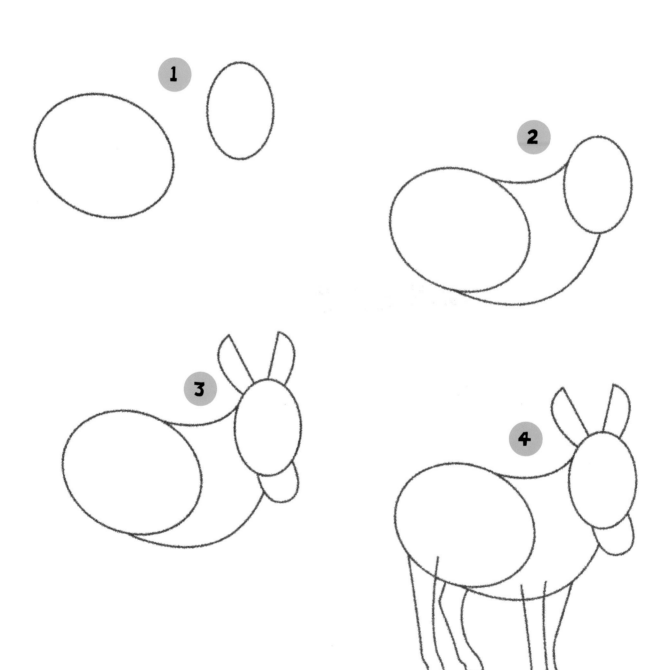

Turkey

Turkeys have wide, squat bodies and short beaks. Male turkeys have long, red wattles below their beaks and down their necks. A turkey will raise its tail and fan its feathers to appear larger and more powerful.

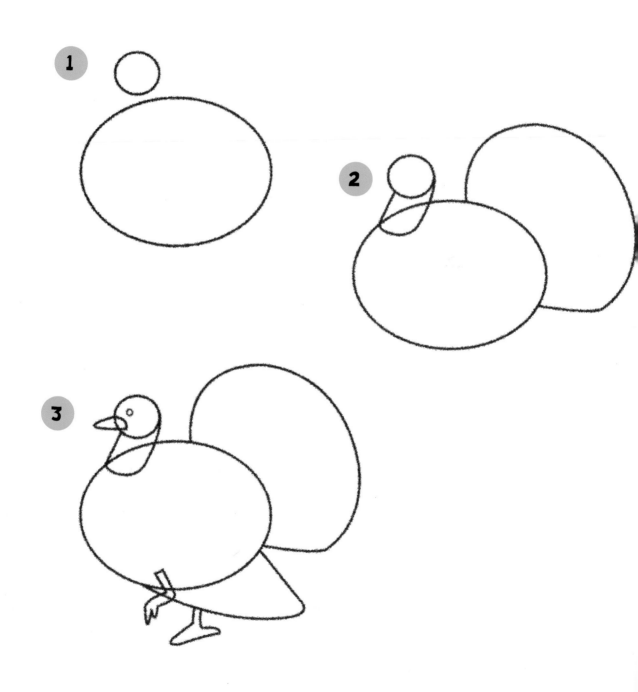

Fun Fact

Female turkeys are not as colorful as the larger, showy males. Most females have brown feathers with some white and light stripes. Males have vivid tail feathers—which are often black and amber with spots of gold and green—to intimidate other male turkeys and to attract females.

Rooster

The rooster guards the hen house.
It sits high on a perch so it can see intruders
and warn hens of impending danger with
its distinctive alarm, "cocka-doodle-doo!"

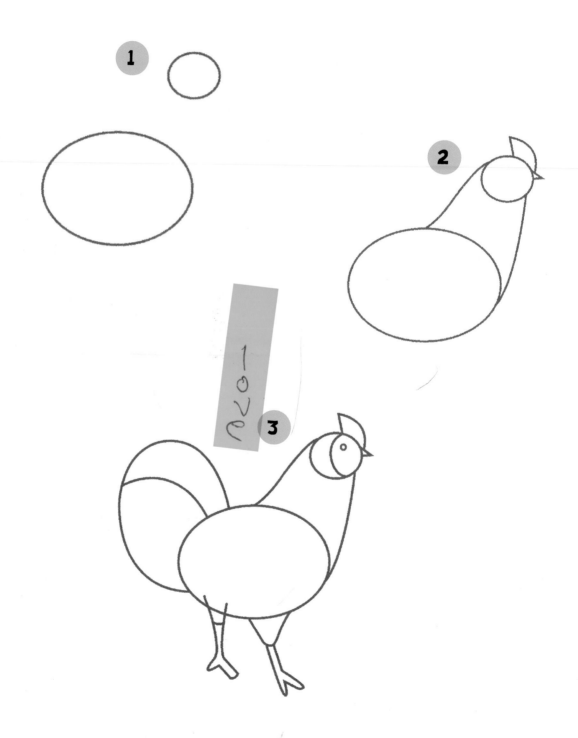

Fun Fact

The rooster's distinctive head consists of earlobes; a wattle that hangs from its beak; and a crest, or comb, on the top of its head—all of which are usually bright red.

Chicken

chickens provide farmers with plenty
of fresh eggs. Hens love to feed on worms,
insects, grains, corn, and other vegetables
to give them the energy they need to lay eggs.

Baby Chick

Baby chicks have soft, fluffy feathers that are not sufficient enough to keep their bodies warm. For the first five weeks of its life, a chick cannot go outdoors and must be kept warm at all times.

Fun Fact

Not all baby chicks are yellow. They are often white, spotted brown, or even black. A chick's feathers will not change color as it ages, so its feathers as a chick will be the color of its feathers as a full-grown chicken!

Duck

This waterfowl lives on the farm's pond or stream. A duck's webbed feet act like little underwater paddles, making it an excellent swimmer and causing it to waddle when it walks.

Fun Fact

Ducks have special feathers that are covered in a layer of oil, making them waterproof. The soft inner feathers stay dry, keeping the ducks nice and warm.

Duckling

Ducklings spend the first few weeks of life following their mother's every move. This is how they learn where to find food, where to swim, and how long to swim before their feathers absorb too much water.

Fun Fact

Ducklings are usually born in the spring through early summer. That's because female ducks lay more eggs when the daylight is longer.

Cat

Farm cats are always busy prowling for small pests. Farmers appreciate them for keeping the vermin under control. In return, these frisky fellas receive a warm place to sleep and plenty of fresh milk!

Field Mouse

The mouse has large, round ears and a long tail. Field Mice love taking advantage of the loose seeds and food scraps that can be found around the farm and on the barn floor.

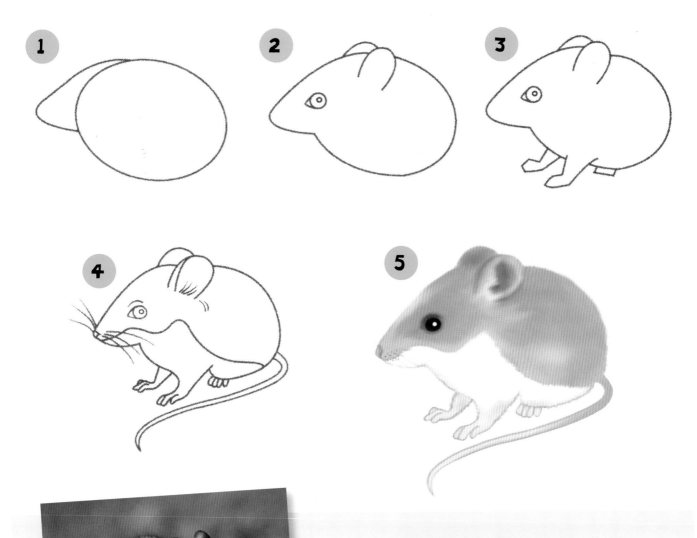

1

2

3

4

5

Fun Fact

This sneaky rodent is tough to catch. Its eyesight is best at night; therefore, these nocturnal beings are rarely seen—let alone caught—during the day.

Goose

on the farm, a goose is never alone.
Geese travel in packs called gaggles, which
keep them safe from predators and allow
them to fly in a "v" formation during migrations.

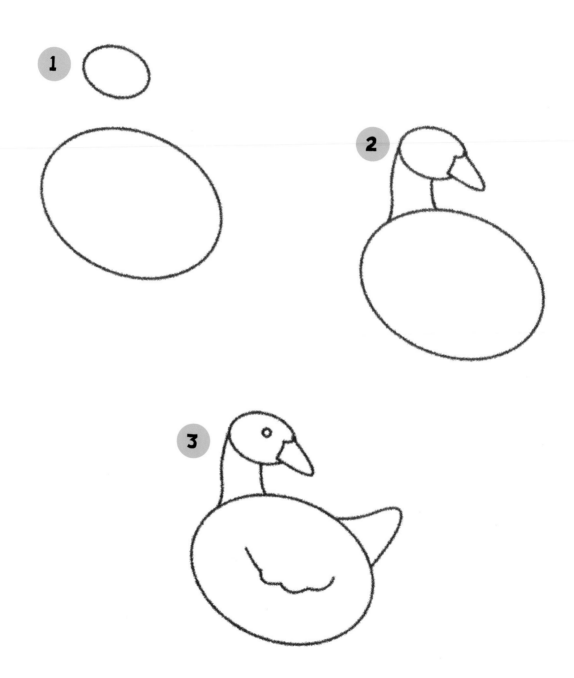

4

5

Fun Fact

The name "goose" actually denotes the female gender of this species. Males are called ganders, and chicks are called goslings.

6

Border Collie

The Border collie is the farmer's loyal companion. This dog's shaggy fur helps keep it warm in the winter and cool in the summer. Because of its natural instinct to corral a pack, this herding dog helps the farmer drive sheep and cattle.

Fun Fact

Border Collies are often referred to as the most intelligent of the dog breeds. They love being active and often perform in agility contests where they must use their skill and intellect to help them navigate through obstacle courses.

Alpaca

The alpaca is a relative of the llama and the camel. Farmers raise them for their long, soft fleece, which is used to create supple yarn that can be spun or woven into blankets and clothing.

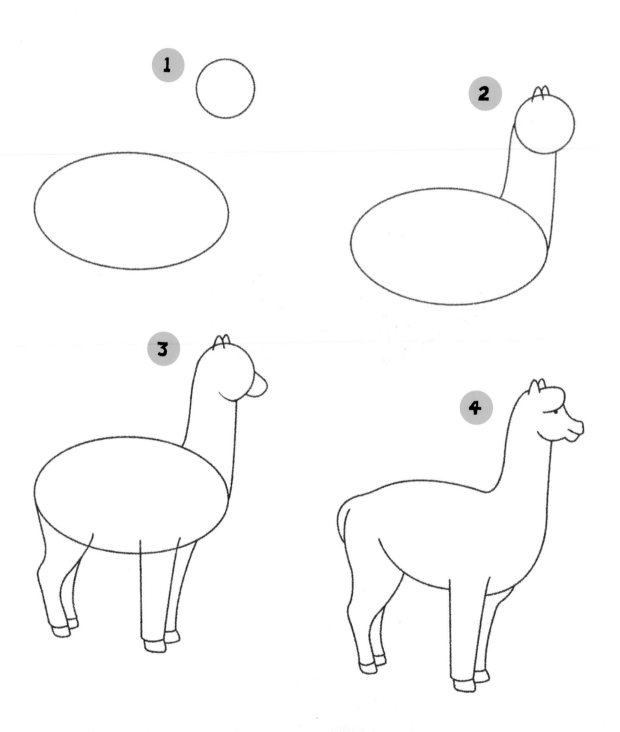

Fun Fact

Alpaca fleece is prized not only for its soft, silky hair-like quality but also because alpacas come in a variety of shades—more than 50 in all!

Rabbit

No farm is complete without a few families
of rabbits. Their long ears give them
a keen sense of hearing, while their powerful
hind legs give them the strength to make a speedy
getaway—their best form of self-defense.

Fun Fact

Rabbits are herbivores and love to graze on grass and leafy greens. As a result, they are sometimes considered a nuisance because they may forage on young crops and can quickly eat their way through entire fields.

Ostrich

This large, flightless bird originated in Africa. Some farmers raise ostriches for their eggs and feathers, which are used for decoration. This bird has long, powerful legs and a long neck, which allows it to spot predators.